D0833753

Colour Songs and Rhymes

Illustrated by Geoffrey Butcher.

In this book and accompanying extended play record, all the colours of the rainbow are presented to children for their information and enjoyment. Young children can learn about colours in many ways; when they are dressing and undressing, when they are working with their toys, when they are out and about using their eyes and asking questions.

To sing songs and chant rhymes about colours helps to increase their awareness of colour and reinforce the knowledge they are gaining. This is not only pleasurable, but is a basic skill which will be very valuable later at school when learning to describe things and identify similarities and differences.

At the back of the book you will find additional notes for parents or teachers about the rhymes.

Macdonald Educational Ltd.

Colour Songs and Rhymes

First published 1974 by
Three Four Five Publishing Ltd.
This edition published 1979 by
Macdonald Educational Ltd.
Holywell House, Worship St, London EC2

© Macdonald Educational Ltd. 1974

Made and printed in Great Britain by W. S. Cowell Ltd., Ipswich.

ISBN 0 903016 29 X

Roses are red

Roses are red, violets are blue,
Sugar is sweet, and so are you.

I've got a fine new kite

I've got a fine new kite, scarlet bright,
Tail a-trailing, blow wind and toss it, please,
Over the trees, far a-sailing.

I've got a fine new kite, lemon bright,
Tail a-trailing, blow wind and toss it, please,
Over the trees, far a-sailing.

I've got a fine new kite, purple bright,
Tail a-trailing, blow wind and toss it, please,
Over the trees, far a-sailing.

I've got a fine new kite, emerald bright,
Tail a-trailing, blow wind and toss it, please,
Over the trees, far a-sailing.

Hector Protector

Hector Protector was dressed all in green,
Hector Protector was sent to the queen.
The queen did not like him, no more did the king,
So Hector Protector was sent back again.

5

White sand and grey sand

White sand and grey sand.
Who'll buy my grey sand?
Who'll buy my white sand?

Brown sand and yellow sand.
Who'll buy my yellow sand?
Who'll buy my brown sand?

Red sand and orange sand.
Who'll buy my orange sand?
Who'll buy my red sand?

6

Jolly red nose

Nose, nose, jolly red nose,
And what gave thee that jolly red nose?
Nutmeg and ginger, cinnamon and cloves,
That's what gave me this jolly red nose.

Rainbow

Rainbow glowing in the sky,
Rainbow flowers are growing by.
Violet, indigo, red and blue,
Colours of the rainbow's hue.
Yellow, orange, soft fresh green,
All the colours to be seen.
Rainbow glowing in the sky,
Rainbow flowers are growing by.

9

It's snowing, it's blowing

It's snowing, it's blowing,
But I am safe from harm,
For I shall wear a yellow pair
Of gloves to keep me warm.

It's snowing, it's blowing,
But I am safe from harm,
For I shall wear a lilac pair
Of pants to keep me warm.

It's snowing, it's blowing,
But I am safe from harm,
For I shall wear an orange pair
Of socks to keep me warm.

It's snowing, it's blowing,
But I am safe from harm,
For I shall wear a purple pair
Of boots to keep me warm.

Watch my hens

Watch my hens and you will see,
They walk always one, two, three.
First the black one leads the line,
Then the white with feathers fine.
Brownie follows last, and she
Makes the third one, you will see.

Brown potatoes

Brown potatoes, white potatoes,
Change them if you can.
Turn them into golden chips,
Frying in the pan.

13

Green, green, green

Green, green, green, is everything I'm wearing,
Green, green, green, my only clothes shall be.
Why do I always dress myself in green?
Because a forester is the one I love.

Blue, blue, blue, is everything I'm wearing,
Blue, blue, blue, my only clothes shall be.
Why do I always dress myself in blue?
Because a sailor is the one I love.

Red, red, red, is everything I'm wearing,
Red, red, red, my only clothes shall be.
Why do I always dress myself in red?
Because a fireman is the one I love.

Black, black, black, is everything I'm wearing,
Black, black, black, my only clothes shall be.
Why do I always dress myself in black?
Because a miner is the one I love.

White, white, white, is everything I'm wearing,
White, white, white, my only clothes shall be.
Why do I always dress myself in white?
Because a baker is the one I love.

Bright, bright, bright, is everything I'm wearing,
Bright, bright, bright, my only clothes shall be.
Why do I always dress in bright colours?
Because an artist is the one I love.

15

Tick tack too

Tick tack too,
Mend a lady's shoe.
A red shoe, a red shoe,
Tick tack too.

Tick tack too,
Mend a man's shoe.
A black shoe, a black shoe,
Tick tack too.

Tick tack too,
Mend a baby's shoe.
A pink shoe, a pink shoe,
Tick tack too.

Tick tack too,
Mend a boy's shoe.
A brown shoe, a brown shoe,
Tick tack too.

Tick tack too,
Mend a girl's shoe.
A blue shoe, a blue shoe,
Tick tack too.

Farmer Howe

Farmer Howe, farmer Howe,
Farmer Howe has one brown cow.

Farmer Penn, farmer Penn,
Farmer Penn has one white hen.

Farmer Mogg, farmer Mogg,
Farmer Mogg has one black hog.

Farmer Beddow, farmer Beddow,
Farmer Beddow has one green meadow.

Farmer Higgs, farmer Higgs,
Farmer Higgs has ten pink pigs.

Lavender's blue

Lavender's blue diddle, diddle,
Lavender's green,
When I am king, diddle, diddle,
You shall be queen.

Call up your men diddle, diddle,
Set them to work,
Some to the plough, diddle, diddle,
Some to the cart.

Some to make hay diddle, diddle,
Some to cut corn,
While you and I, diddle, diddle,
Keep ourselves warm.

Lavender's blue diddle, diddle,
Lavender's green,
When I am king, diddle, diddle,
You shall be queen.

Ripe cherries

Come, let's go and gather ripe cherries,
I know a place where many grow.
Red and black and white and golden,
One, two, three, on every row.
Val-e-ri,   Val-e-ra.
Val-e-ri,   Val-e-ra.
One, two and three on every row.

Bubbles from my pipe

Bubbles from my pipe I blow,
Red, yellow, in the air,
Orange, green, off they go,
Blue, white, everywhere.

Bubbles from my pipe I blow,
Pink, violet, in the air,
Red, purple, off they go,
Rainbows, everywhere.

Notes:

Colours are everywhere! These songs and rhymes give constant opportunity to point away from the book to colours in the house, in the garden, in clothes, toys, crayons, magazines and so on. All of this reinforces the knowledge gained, encourages an understanding of the benefit of learning, and adds excitement to the constant process of discovery.

Children who have learned the songs and rhymes in this book will start to notice colour, and will start to use words like *'tan', 'gold', 'silver'* and *'navy blue'*, far beyond its scope. The thing to remember is that this is all building awareness, vocabulary, initiative and will develop a valuable sense of comparison and fitness, skills which will be of enormous value at school.

Colour blindness:

Many parents worry about colour blindness in their children, and their worry is usually groundless. Nevertheless very occasionally colour blindness does exist, probably then over only a small range of the spectrum.

It is far better to know about it and be able to allow for it than to ignore it.

Some other Three Four Five products:

Create a Story Books
'Flip-over' books which provide children with opportunity both to make up stories and to make things happen. Each book has twenty-four full colour pages, which a child can flip over to make up as many as 2401 different picture stories.

Jigbits Unique three-dimensional jigsaws with thick, double-sided pieces which slot together to make stand-up figures. Designs include Animals, Men, Circus and Legends.

Record Books A series of books containing traditional rhymes and songs, illustrated in full colour. Each book includes an E.P. record of children singing the rhymes and songs.

Board Games A range of well-designed, entertaining games for the very young which encourage recognition, matching of shapes and colours and give practice at counting.

Three Four Five Nursery Course - the play school through the post.

A complete year's programme of enjoyable yet stimulating activities designed to develop in your child the basic skills that lead to reading, writing, number sense and self expression. It comes through the post in twelve colourful monthly packs.

Each pack, presented in book form, contains games, puzzles, cut-outs, stories and a double sided 45 rpm 7″ record of songs and action rhymes recorded by young children. There are also eight pages of notes each month with additional ideas, suggestions and play activities.

"A cleverly worked out scheme to encourage the development of all the young child's faculties"
The Times.

For a FREE colour brochure please write to:
345 Nursery Course Administrator
Macdonald Educational Ltd, Holywell House.
Worship St. London EC2

Australia: 3/4/5 Nursery Course, World Record Club Pty. Ltd. P.O. Box 76, Burwood, Victoria 3125.

Canada: 3/4/5 Nursey Course, Setsco Educational Ltd. 567 Clarke Rd., Quitlam, British Columbia V3J 3X4.

South Africa: 3/4/5 Nursery Course (Pty) Ltd., P.O. Box 67744, Bryanston, Transvaal.